# BIOGRAPHIC
# BOWIE

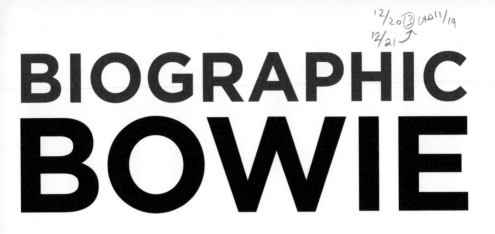

# BIOGRAPHIC
# BOWIE

**LIZ FLAVELL**

AMMONITE
**PRESS**

First published 2018 by
Ammonite Press
an imprint of Guild of Master Craftsman Publications Ltd
Castle Place, 166 High Street, Lewes, East Sussex, BN7 1XU,
United Kingdom
www.ammonitepress.com

ISBN 978 1 78145 327 8

Publisher: Jason Hook
Concept Design: Matt Carr
Design & Illustration: Matt Carr & Robin Shields
Editor: Jamie Pumfrey

Colour reproduction by GMC Reprographics
Printed and bound in China

# CONTENTS

# ICONOGRAPHIC

WHEN WE CAN RECOGNIZE A MUSICIAN BY A SET OF ICONS, WE CAN ALSO RECOGNIZE HOW COMPLETELY THAT ARTIST AND THEIR MUSIC HAVE ENTERED OUR CULTURE AND OUR CONSCIOUSNESS.

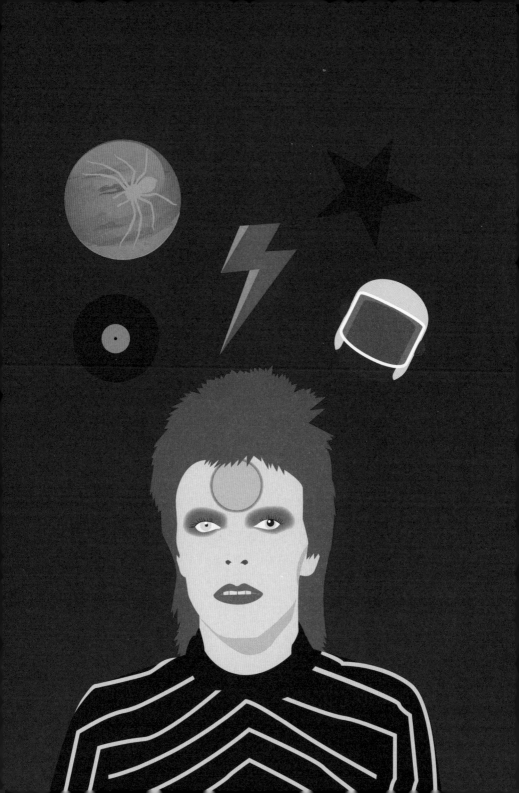

# INTRODUCTION

The task of trying to convey the essence of David Bowie through 50 icons and infographics is an appealingly impossible one. His life defied stereotypes and conventions, his art resisted categorization, and the boundary between both was always blurred. Bowie was a chameleon: by turns musician, actor, artist and style icon, appearing and performing as spaceman, glitter king, soul boy, recluse, raconteur, addict, teetotaller, lover, husband, father – but constantly a cultural revolutionary, making successive generations of music fans believe in the possibility of being heroes.

The death of David Bowie on 10 January 2016 was particularly shocking as just two days before – on his 69th birthday – he had surprised fans with the release of his 25th studio album *Blackstar*. The idea that he could have died from cancer, so soon after such a powerful and creative comeback, seemed impossible. Key motifs – Bowie as a being from beyond this planet, the sense of a choreographed life, the fusing of life and art – were brilliantly reinforced in a final artistic act that prompted a global outpouring of grief and secured his legacy.

"I ALWAYS HAD A REPULSIVE SORT OF NEED TO BE SOMETHING MORE THAN HUMAN."

—David Bowie, *Rolling Stone*, 12 February 1976

David Bowie's life began normally enough. He was born David Jones, in the austere atmosphere of post-war suburban London. Like many young people of the time, he became enamoured of American music and the sounds of Little Richard and Elvis. David Jones possessed a fierce drive to live a life less ordinary, whether as artist, actor or musician. He dabbled in everything that London in the Swinging Sixties had to offer, including mime classes, meditation with Buddhist monks, folk festivals and all-night orgies.

By 1969, he had changed his name to David Bowie and 'Space Oddity' had become the soundtrack to the moon landing. He had launched his career at a time when the world was soaring beyond traditional boundaries, and rocketed to true stardom with his creation of Ziggy Stardust. Dressed as a flame-haired space refugee, Bowie electrified audiences with avant-garde performances and sounds. Best-selling albums *Hunky Dory*, *The Rise and Fall of Ziggy Stardust and the Spiders from Mars* and *Aladdin Sane* became guiding stars for a generation of displaced kids. If you seemed a little different, the gender-bending, role-playing Bowie made it feel okay.

Bowie's alter egos and musical experiments punctuated successive rock and pop eras. From the enigmatic Thin White Duke of the Berlin and electronica years to the tanned, blond, bouffant Bowie of 'Let's Dance' disco, his reinventions reinforced his relevance. His final album, *Blackstar*, is in many ways the most astonishing. As news of Bowie's death was announced, the true significance of the album became apparent. The ambiguous lyrics, symbolic videos and metamorphosing album art were Bowie's unique way of exploring his mortality and saying goodbye. His death, like his life, had become a work of art.

## "SOMETIMES YOU WILL NEVER KNOW THE TRUE VALUE OF A MOMENT UNTIL IT BECOMES A MEMORY."

—Iman Abdulmajid,
9 January 2016

Bowie's cultural impact was felt far beyond even such influential songs as 'Life On Mars?' and era-defining movies like *The Man Who Fell To Earth*. Who knew the Internet would change our world? Bowie did in 1999. Who dressed like a woman to shake up ideas of gender? That was Bowie in 1971, kicking up controversy about his sexuality. For many fans, Bowie was much more than a rock star – he opened a door that set people free to be whatever they wanted. Our infographic celebration of his life and world, work and legacy, attempts to capture at least some of the earthly masks and personas, icons and inventions, of the artist that will be remembered as the 'Starman'.

# 01
## LIFE

# "I'VE ALWAYS THOUGHT THE ONLY THING TO DO WAS TO TRY TO GO THROUGH LIFE AS SUPERMAN, RIGHT FROM THE WORD GO. I FELT FAR TOO INSIGNIFICANT AS JUST ANOTHER PERSON."

—David Bowie, *Playboy*, September 1976

# DAVID BOWIE

## was born on 8 January 1947 in Brixton, London

LONDON

BRIXTON

David Robert Jones was born in London at 40 Stansfield Road, Brixton. His father, Haywood Stenton 'John' Jones, was a public relations officer for the children's charity Dr Barnardo's and had met Bowie's mother, Margaret Mary 'Peggy' Burns, when she was working as a waitress. Peggy already had a son called Terry and another child who had been put up for adoption. John had a wife and a little girl. John and Peggy didn't tie the knot until David was eight months old, when John's divorce was finalized.

Two years after the end of the Second World War, rationing was still in effect and food was scarce. The Jones's three-storey terraced house was shared with two other families. Outside, the streets were grey and children played on bomb sites, but it was out of the ashes of this war-stressed city that Bowie rose.

UNITED KINGDOM

### GRANDFATHER

**James Edward Burns**
(1887-1946)

### GRANDMOTHER

**Mary Heaton**
(1880–d. unknown)

Peggy's first son and Bowie's half-brother, Terry Burns, was born in 1937. Peggy also had a brief affair during the war and had a baby she called Myra Ann Burns. The girl was put up for adoption in 1943.

### MOTHER

**Margaret Mary 'Peggy' Burns**
(1913-2001)

### WIFE

**Mary Angela 'Angie' Barnett**
(1949–)

*Married in 1970 and divorced in 1980*

### SON

**Duncan Zowie Haywood Jones**
(1971–)

**David Robert Jones**
(1947-2016)

# BOWIE'S FAMILY TREE

Bowie's grandfather Robert Jones was only 34 years old when he was killed in the Battle of the Somme; his wife Zillah died just four months later and Bowie's father was raised by an aunt. John had a strong bond with his son, but he died before he saw him succeed. In contrast, Bowie had a problematic relationship with his mother and spent a number of years out of contact, before reconciling in 1992. Bowie's half-brother Terry was his childhood hero, but he struggled with mental illness and spent time in an institute before committing suicide in 1985.

### GRANDFATHER

**Robert Haywood Jones**
(1882–1916)

### GRANDMOTHER

**Zillah Hannah Blackburn**
(1887–1917)

### FATHER

**Haywood Stenton 'John' Jones**
(1912–69)

Bowie's half-sister Annette was born in 1941, the result of his father's fling with a nurse during the war. Annette was raised by John's first wife, Hilda.

### WIFE

**Iman Abdulmajid**
(1955–)

*Married in 1992*

### DAUGHTER

**Alexandria Zahra Jones**
(2000–)

# SWINGING SIXTIES

## 1962

🍸 George Underwood, Bowie's best friend, punches him in the face in a disagreement over a girl. The punch causes Bowie's mismatched eyes.

🎵 Bowie and Underwood form The Konrads, with Bowie on the sax and backing vocals. They play covers of The Beatles and The Shadows.

## 1966

🎵 Bowie is taken under the wing of showbiz manager Ken Pitt. By the end of the year, Pitt has got Bowie a contract with Decca's new label, Deram.

🍸 Bowie visits Pitt's home, and borrows from his copious library – Oscar Wilde and Albert Camus fire his imagination.

## 1965

🍸 To avoid confusion with Davy Jones, singer with The Monkees, Davie Jones becomes David Bowie, after the American pioneer James 'Jim' Bowie.

## 1967

🎵 Bowie releases his first album, *David Bowie,* on 1 June. The week before, *Sgt. Pepper's Lonely Hearts Club Band* by The Beatles is released.

🍸 Increasingly fascinated by Buddhism, Bowie heads to a retreat in Scotland where he considers becoming a monk. In August, Bowie meets dancer and mime artist Lindsay Kemp and enrols at his dance centre in Covent Garden, London. In September, Bowie appears in his first film *The Image*. By October, Bowie has received his Equity card, signifying membership of the British entertainment professionals' trade union.

## LIFESTYLE
## MUSIC

### 1963

Bowie leaves school with one O level in art. His teacher Owen Frampton finds him work as a trainee commercial artist/visualizer.

The Konrads record the song 'I Never Dreamed' for Decca, but it is unsuccessful. Bowie takes the name Davie Jones.

### 1965

Bowie joins the mod band The Lower Third and takes up residency at the Marquee Club. The band uses an old ambulance to travel to gigs.

### 1964

London is swinging and Bowie soaks it all up.

Bowie forms R&B band The King Bees. Single 'Liza Jane' fails to chart, so he leaves the band.

### 1968

Bowie auditions for the musical *Hair*. In April, on the set of a BBC production of *Theatre 625,* he meets ballet dancer Hermione Farthingale.

Bowie and Farthingale form a band called Turquoise, later changed to Feathers, and play light 'n' fluffy 1960s songs.

### 1969

Bowie starts a folk club called the Arts Lab, hosted at the Three Tuns pub in Beckenham. On 5 August, Bowie's father dies.

In the year of the moon landing, Bowie scores his first hit with 'Space Oddity'. The song goes to number five in the UK charts and earns him a joint Ivor Novello award.

# TURN AND FACE THE STRANGE

From a young age, Bowie was very striking.
He was skeletally thin and his unique eyes
produced a mesmeric gaze.

## MAKEUP

Aged three, Bowie was caught putting on makeup by his mum. She told him he looked like a clown.

## EYES

George Underwood's punch to Bowie's face damaged his iris sphincter muscle. This injury led to anisocoria, which made his pupils appear to be different sizes and sometimes made his eyes look different colours.

## TEETH

Throughout the 1970s, the Bowie smile shone brightly despite his infamous wonky teeth. German artist Jessine Hein found them so fascinating that she made a hand-sculpted recreation of his original teeth. Bowie finally underwent dental work in the 1980s, before going for a full set of new teeth in the 1990s.

# HAIR

Bowie's first television appearance was when he was 17 years old. As president of the Society for the Prevention of Cruelty to Long-Haired Men, Bowie was featured on the BBC *Tonight* programme, sporting a long, blond hairdo.

# CIGARETTES

Bowie's addiction to cigarettes was legendary and it began when he was a teenager. For many years he puffed away at around 80 cigarettes a day. Interviews with the star were conducted under a fog of heavy smoke. If you listen carefully to the song 'Can You Hear Me' from *Young Americans* you can hear him take a quick puff. It took a series of heart attacks for him to kick the habit for good.

# LEFT-HANDED

Bowie was left-handed for writing but right-handed for playing guitar.

# BOWIE'S LONDON

Bowie spent his early life and career in London. Though he was born in Brixton and often referred to himself as a "Brixton boy", in 1953 the Jones's withdrew ten miles south to the London Borough of Bromley. Bowie lived there for ten years, until, aged 16, he migrated back to central London for his first and only job in the real world at the Nevin D. Hirst Advertising Agency.

In the pursuit of fame and fortune, Bowie threw himself into his music, playing gigs across the capital and making Soho his home. In 1974, less than six months after retiring Ziggy Stardust, he left the city permanently.

**DECCA STUDIOS**
Recorded first album, *David Bowie*, and the 1967 single 'The Laughing Gnome'.

**BBC TELEVISION CENTRE**
Filmed 'Starman' for *Top of the Pops* in 1972.

**HAMMERSMITH APOLLO**
Announced the end of Ziggy Stardust in 1973.

## GLOBAL REAL ESTATE

After leaving London, Bowie's success gave him the opportunity to live all over the world.

New York City, USA (1974–75)
Los Angeles, USA (1975–76)
Berlin, Germany (1976–78)
Vaud, Switzerland (1976–82)
New York City, USA (1979)
Lausanne, Switzerland (1982–92)
Sydney, Australia (1982–92)
Mustique, West Indies (1989–95)
New York City, USA (1992–2002)
Somerset, Bermuda (1997)
New York City, USA (1999–2016)
Ulster County, USA (2003–16)

**KEY**

- Home
- Performance
- Social
- Studio
- Photo shoot

**TRIDENT STUDIOS**
Recorded *David Bowie*, *Hunky Dory* and *The Rise and Fall of Ziggy Stardust and the Spiders from Mars*.

**VALE COURT**
Lived for six months in 1973.

**LA GIOCONDA**
Met with Marc Bolan and Steve Marriott to discuss music.

**39 MANCHESTER STREET**
Lodged with manager Ken Pitt in 1967.

**MARQUEE CLUB**
Filmed *The 1980 Floor Show* in 1973.

**22 CLAREVILLE GROVE**
Lived with Hermione Farthingale in 1968.

**CARNABY STREET**
Foraged through shop bins for cast-off clothes.

**HEDDON STREET**
Posed for the cover of *Ziggy Stardust* in 1972.

**89 OAKLEY STREET**
Lived 1973–4.

**40 STANSFIELD ROAD**
Born and raised until six years old.

**43 GILSTON ROAD**
Bought mansion in Chelsea, but never lived in it due to harassment from the paparazzi.

CAMDEN

WESTMINSTER

LAMBETH

LIFE

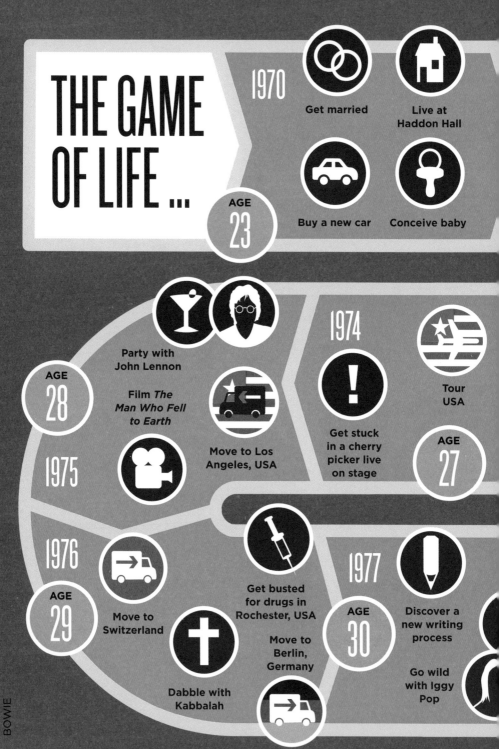

# THE GAME OF LIFE ...

**1970**

**AGE 23**

Get married

Live at Haddon Hall

Buy a new car

Conceive baby

Party with John Lennon

Film *The Man Who Fell to Earth*

Move to Los Angeles, USA

**1974**

Get stuck in a cherry picker live on stage

Tour USA

**AGE 27**

**AGE 28**

**1975**

**1976**

**AGE 29**

Move to Switzerland

Dabble with Kabbalah

Get busted for drugs in Rochester, USA

Move to Berlin, Germany

**1977**

**AGE 30**

Discover a new writing process

Go wild with Iggy Pop

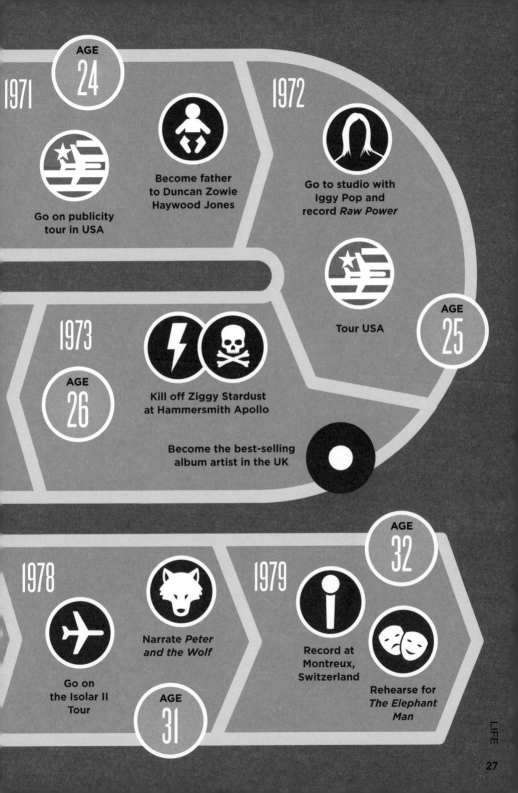

**1971**

AGE **24**

Go on publicity
tour in USA

Become father
to Duncan Zowie
Haywood Jones

**1972**

Go to studio with
Iggy Pop and
record *Raw Power*

Tour USA

AGE **25**

**1973**

AGE **26**

Kill off Ziggy Stardust
at Hammersmith Apollo

Become the best-selling
album artist in the UK

**1978**

Go on
the Isolar II
Tour

Narrate *Peter
and the Wolf*

AGE **31**

**1979**

Record at
Montreux,
Switzerland

AGE **32**

Rehearse for
*The Elephant
Man*

# JANUARY

January was a significant month throughout Bowie's life. It was the month of his birth, death and much more ...

**4**
1973
'The Jean Genie' is aired on *Top of the Pops*

**5**
2015
Asteroid is named 342843 Davidbowie

**10**
2016
Death

**11**
1972
Performs on BBC Radio 1 for DJ John Peel

**16**
1985
Half-brother Terry Burns commits suicide

**17**
1996
Inducted into the Rock and Roll Hall of Fame

**23**
1971
Arrives in the USA for the first time

1976
Releases *Station to Station*

**24**
1973
Adds finishing touches to *Aladdin Sane*

**29**
1972
Performs at Friars Aylesbury – Freddie Mercury is in the audience

**1974**
Demos tracks at Olympic Studios, London

**3**
**1973**
Records 'The Jean Genie' for *Top of the Pops*

**1972**
Releases 'Changes'

**8**
**1947** Birth

**2016**
Releases *Blackstar*

**14**
**1966**
Releases 'Can't Help Thinking About Me'
**1977**
Releases *Low*

**15**
**1971**
Releases 'Holy Holy'
**2016**
*Blackstar* debuts at Number 1 in UK

**25**
**2010**
Releases live album *A Reality Tour*

**26**
**1975**
Alan Yentob's Bowie film *Cracked Actor* is aired

**27**
**1983**
Signs contract with EMI America

**1**
**1970**
Travels to Edinburgh to work on *The Looking Glass Murders*

Music

Personal

Other

# MODERN LOVE

David Bowie's love life was as experimental and progressive as his music. He was married twice and had a string of high-profile liaisons, with even Elizabeth Taylor supposedly falling for his charms. In 1972, just two years after marrying American model Angie Barnett, Bowie announced that he was gay. He later revised this to bisexual, before changing his mind again by stating, "I was always a closet heterosexual." In a 2002 interview, after years of rumours about his sexual prowess, Bowie declared: "I was incredibly promiscuous and I think we'll leave it at that."

## HERMIONE FARTHINGALE

The red-haired hippy and actress was the first love of Bowie's life. In the summer of 1968, he moved into her flat in South Kensington. Bowie rarely wrote personal lyrics, but he later opened his heart in the songs 'Letter to Hermione' and 'An Occasional Dream'.

## 1968

## 1969

After Hermione, Bowie retreated to Beckenham and into the arms of his landlady Mary Finnigan. Together, they formed the Arts Lab at the Three Tuns pub and Bowie played her his music.

## MARY FINNIGAN

# 1970

## MARY ANGELA 'ANGIE' BARNETT

Exuberant, Swiss-educated, a multi-sexually orientated blast of charged energy, it was Angie who found Haddon Hall and transformed it into a palatial home for her creative husband. As their open marriage fell apart, he likened the relationship to "living with a blowtorch".

# 1990

## IMAN ABDULMAJID

"I was naming the children the night we met." Bowie never made a secret that it was love at first sight when he was introduced to Iman at a party in 1990. The Somali supermodel was more than an intellectual match for Bowie and they married in April 1992. In August 2000, the couple had a daughter, Alexandria.

# 1987

In 1987, while on the Glass Spider Tour, Bowie met American ballet dancer Melissa Hurley. They were engaged in 1990, but Bowie broke it off when he realized that the 20-year age difference would become a problem in the future.

## MELISSA HURLEY

# DEATH
## 10 JANUARY 2016

Mike Garson, Bowie's long-standing pianist, claims Bowie was told by a psychic in the late 1970s that he would die aged "69 or 70" – he confided that it was something that Bowie truly believed. In his final photo shoot, on his 69th birthday, Bowie seemed playful and happy.

*"I'D LIKE MY DEATH TO BE AS INTERESTING AS MY LIFE HAS BEEN AND WILL BE."*

—David Bowie, *Playboy*, September 1976

*"HIS DEATH WAS NO DIFFERENT FROM HIS LIFE – A WORK OF ART."*

—Tony Visconti, Bowie's friend and producer, 11 January 2016

Taken by friend and photographer Jimmy King, the photos were posted on Bowie's Instagram account, with the caption: "Why is this man so happy? Is it because it's his 69th birthday or that he's released his 28th studio album today and it's a corker?"

Two days later, Bowie died in his New York apartment, having privately suffered with liver cancer for the previous 18 months. Fans around the world mourned their hero. In Brixton's Windrush Square, the crowd sang along to 'Starman' and 'Let's Dance'. In New York, flowers were piled at the doors of 285 Lafayette Street, where Bowie had spent his final days. In Berlin, people gathered outside Hauptstrasse 155, in the district of Schöneberg, where Bowie shared a flat with Iggy Pop from 1976 to 1978. Bowie was cremated with no funeral service and his final resting place is known only to his closest family.

DAVID
BOWIE

## 02
# WORLD

# "YOU'RE TALKING ABOUT A RATHER WORLDLY, KNOWLEDGEABLE YOUNG BUCK WHO WAS READY TO GO OUT INTO THE WORLD AND SHOOT HIS BOLT. BUT WHO WAS FOCUSED ON A PARTICULAR TARGET — SUCCESS."

—Iggy Pop, *Starman*, 2012

# INSPIRATIONS FOR AN ICON

When the doors opened to the *David Bowie Is* exhibition at the Victoria and Albert Museum in London in 2013, one of the first displays was a replica of Bowie's bedroom when he was growing up. It was drab and dark, but it harboured his childhood inspirations ...

## SKETCH PAD

At Bromley Technical High School, form teacher and art master Owen Frampton (father of musician Peter Frampton) had an enormous impact on young Bowie. He encouraged his pupils to think about their future careers and diverted many of them towards art school. David Bowie often claimed he went to art school even though he didn't.

## TELEVISION

In 1953, John Jones bought a TV so that the family could watch the coronation of Queen Elizabeth II, but the six-year-old Bowie was far more interested in watching a black-and-white drama on the BBC called *The Quatermass Experiment*. This classic series sparked a lifelong fascination with science fiction.

## RECORD PLAYER

Young Bowie loved jazz and was transfixed by Little Richard. When asked about hearing his 1955 hit 'Tutti Frutti', Bowie replied: "It filled the room with energy and colour and outrageous defiance. I had heard God."

**LITTLE RICHARD**

'Tutti Frutti'

## AMERICAN FOOTBALL

In the 1950s, a short-wave radio was like a passport to another world. Bowie spent hours listening to the US Armed Forces Radio and American sports commentary. He became obsessed with American football and enjoyed looking at photographs of the players in their kits. In November 1960, Bowie was photographed for the *Bromley & Kentish Times* wearing his own bit of kit – it was his first-ever publicity shot!

WORLD

# LIFE ON CARS

## MERCEDES

Bowie once said that the song 'Always Crashing in the Same Car' from the album *Low* was about a crash he'd had in his Mercedes in Switzerland. However, another version of the song's origination came courtesy of Iggy Pop. The story he told went back to the Berlin days at the height of Bowie's cocaine addiction, when the pair were cruising the city bars. Having spotted a drug dealer that he thought had ripped him off, Bowie proceeded to ram the dealer's car. After the incident, Iggy reported that Bowie started driving around at 70 mph (113 kph) in the underground car park of his hotel shouting at the top of his voice that he wanted to end it all by driving into a wall. Luckily, before he could do it, the car ran out of petrol.

In 1973, at the height of Ziggy Stardust, Bowie could be found behind the wheel of a Rolls-Royce Silver Ghost, a world away from the days of turning up to gigs in an old ambulance. Bowie owned a string of classic vehicles including a Jaguar E-Type, a Ford Mustang and a 21-foot (6.4-metre)-long convertible Mercedes limousine – the car of choice for heads of state and dictators.

# RUPERT THE RILEY

In the early 1970s, Bowie, with the help of a friend, built a 1932 Riley 9 Gamecock. Having spent many hours working on the wooden-framed car, he recorded the song 'Rupert the Riley' to show his appreciation of the vehicle. Not long after, the Riley stalled outside Lewisham Police Station in London. Bowie kept the car in first gear as he attempted to crank it up, but it sprang into life and ran over him, breaking both his legs in the process. After a week in Lewisham Hospital, Bowie decided to sell his beloved motor. In the Ziggy Stardust days, you could see the scars from the accident running along the inside of his right thigh.

# MINI

In 1999, the iconic British car the Mini celebrated its 40th anniversary. To commemorate the occasion, makers BMC approached three British icons, Kate Moss, Paul Smith and David Bowie, to design three unique cars for an exhibition. Paul Smith wrapped his car in his signature multi-coloured stripes, Moss opted for a spider's web theme and Bowie made his own mark with a fully mirrored version of the classic car, windows and all. When interviewed about his contribution, he commented that "the viewer's own image becomes the immediate interface". Bowie's Mini is now a permanent fixture in the BMW Museum in Munich.

# HALLO SPACEBOY

Bowie was intrigued by space. It's a subject he orbited time and time again in music and film.

## EARTH

### Earthling (1997)

Bowie starred as a humanoid alien in the 1976 satirical science-fiction film *The Man Who Fell to Earth*.

## MOON

**'Moonage Daydream' (1972)**
**Serious Moonlight Tour (1983)**

Bowie's son Duncan Jones directed the science-fiction film *Moon* in 2009.

## SPACE

**'Space Oddity' (1969)**
**'Dancing Out in Space' (2013)**

In 2013, astronaut Chris Hadfield performed his own version of 'Space Oddity' while on the International Space Station.

## MARS

**'Life on Mars?' (1971)**
***The Rise and Fall of Ziggy Stardust and the Spiders from Mars* (1972)**

The Spiders from Mars, Bowie's band, took their name from a 1954 mass UFO sighting in Italy. Witnesses reported egg-shaped UFOs showering them with a silver glitter. Official reports explained the incident as a mass of floating silk from migrating spiders caught in the jet stream.

## SATELLITE

**'Looking for Satellites' (1997)**

The Lou Reed song 'Satellite of Love' was written in 1970, while Reed was still in The Velvet Underground. It eventually made it on to the Bowie-produced 1972 album, *Transformer*, with Bowie providing backing vocals on the song.

## UFO

**'Born in a UFO' (2013)**

Bowie and his school friends reportedly published a newsletter on UFOs.

## SPACEMAN

**'Ashes to Ashes' (1980)**
**'Hallo Spaceboy' (1995)**

In 1995, Bowie collaborated with artist Damien Hirst on a spin painting called *BEAUTIFUL, HALLO, SPACE-BOY PAINTING*. It was sold at auction in 2016 for £785,000.

## STAR

**'Starman' (1972)**
**'The Prettiest Star' (1973)**
**'New Killer Star' (2003)**
**'The Stars [Are Out Tonight]' (2013)**
***Blackstar* (2016)**

Ziggy Stardust is Bowie's most iconic persona.

# ZIGGY PLAYED ...

... guitar, saxophone, piano and a range of other instruments. On Christmas Day 1961, Bowie had been given a white Grafton saxophone by his father and managed to convince Ronnie Ross, the top baritone saxophonist in the UK, to give him lessons every Saturday morning. Over a decade later, Bowie was producing for Lou Reed, and Ross was hired to perform on 'Walk on the Wild Side'. After Ross had delivered the perfect solo in one take, Bowie stepped out of the control room and said: "Thanks, Ron. Should I see you at your house on Saturday morning?"

HARMONICA

STYLOPHONE

CELLO

VIOLIN

VIOLA

RECORDER

MANDOLIN

2

The number of recorders that Bowie played on 'Life on Mars'. You can hear the sound of the two recorders playing a high counter-melody in the second verse.

ALTO SAXOPHONE

TENOR SAXOPHONE

GUITAR

PIANO

KEYBOARD

MOUTH HARP

KOTO

**12**

Number of strings on Bowie's guitar of choice. His Hagström 12-string gave 'Space Oddity' its signature sound.

**$46,875**

Price paid at auction for a Takamine 12-string dreadnought electro-acoustic guitar played by Bowie on the 1990 Sound and Vision Tour.

# CREATING ZIGGY

## NAME

The alien superstar's name was purloined from a country singer going by the name of the Legendary Stardust Cowboy. Ziggy was taken from a tailor's shop in London's East End.

## MAKEUP

Bowie was taught to put on makeup by his old mime teacher Lindsay Kemp. Before each show, Bowie spent around two hours getting ready. He sourced intense-coloured powders and creams, imported from India, from a shop in Rome. The white rice powder for Bowie's foundation was from Japan and the gold circle on his forehead was achieved using a German gold base from a shop in New York.

## INSPIRATION

Ziggy was a fusion of characters: a dash of Gene Vincent, a hint of Vince Taylor, a pinch of Iggy Pop, a touch of Marc Bolan, a drop of Lindsay Kemp and a shade of Malcolm McDowell from *A Clockwork Orange.*

## HAIR

Bowie's famous haircut was inspired by model Christine Walton, who was featured in *Vogue* in August 1971. The striking red colour was copied from a model on the cover of *Honey* magazine. Suzi Fussey, who was Bowie's mum's hairdresser in Beckenham, was offered the job of transforming Bowie's look. Fussey became the hairstylist on the Ziggy Stardust Tour and later married guitarist Mick Ronson.

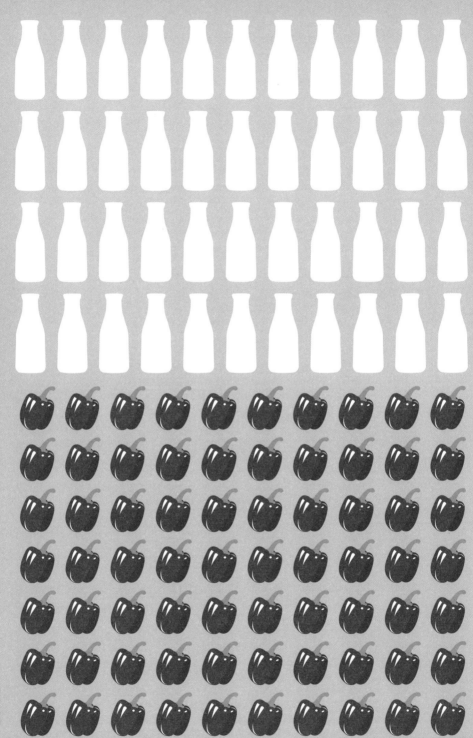

In 1975, Bowie relocated to Los Angeles to star in and provide the soundtrack to *The Man Who Fell to Earth*. After 11 weeks of filming in the New Mexico desert, and having failed to deliver the soundtrack, Bowie returned to the city and started working on his next album. With Ziggy Stardust in retirement, Bowie transformed himself into the Thin White Duke, inspired by his character in *The Man Who Fell to Earth*, and moved into Hollywood's Cherokee Studios.

As the songs began to take shape, fuelled by cocaine addiction, the late nights became days without sleep and Bowie was reportedly sustaining himself on a diet of milk and red peppers. By November, the album *Station to Station* was finished. When interviewed about it years later, Bowie admitted: "I only know it was [recorded] in LA because I've read it was."

# BOWIE LIVED ON A DIET OF MILK AND RED PEPPERS

## 285 LAFAYETTE STREET

Bowie and Iman bought their SoHo penthouse in 1999. They lived there until Bowie's death.

## WASHINGTON SQUARE PARK

Bowie once said that Washington Square Park was his favourite place in the entire city.

## MCNALLY JACKSON BOOKS

Bowie was known for his love of reading and he spent many hours browsing the shelves in his favourite bookstore.

## ESSEX HOUSE HOTEL

Before moving to Lafayette Street, a ninth-floor apartment at the Essex House Hotel was Bowie's home for over a decade.

# NEW YORK'S IN LOVE

In 1993, Bowie settled permanently with Iman in Manhattan. Reverting to his real name of David Jones, he managed to live invisibly – all it took was a cap or a foreign newspaper tucked under his arm to put people off his trail. His daughter Alexandria was born at Mount Sinai Hospital in 2000, and in 2016 he died peacefully at his Manhattan penthouse.

## ELECTRIC CIRCUS

In 1971, Bowie arrived in the USA for the first time. While in New York, he found time to see The Velvet Underground perform at the Electric Circus.

## NEW YORK THEATRE WORKSHOP

One of Bowie's last projects was co-writing *Lazarus*, a musical sequel to *The Man Who Fell to Earth*.

## "I'VE LIVED IN NEW YORK LONGER THAN I'VE LIVED ANYWHERE ELSE. IT'S AMAZING. I AM A NEW YORKER."

—David Bowie, *SOMA*, 2003

WORLD

# THE VISIONARY

Bowie's work went beyond the arts. He was a pioneer in the digital age and even founded his own bank ...

## DOWNLOADABLE

In September 1996, Bowie made history when he released the song 'Telling Lies' for download only on his website. It was the first online single from a major artist and it took over 11 minutes to download. There were 5,000 downloads within the first hours of its launch.

Bowie quit Virgin Records in 2001 to launch his own independent label, ISO. Commenting on the decision, Bowie said: "I've not been in agreement with how things are done and, as a writer of some proliferation, frustrated at how slow and lumbering it all is."

## BOWIE BONDS

In 1997, Bowie became the first musical artist to float on the stock market. 'Bowie Bonds' enabled investors to take a share of the royalties from a back catalogue that included *Hunky Dory*, *Aladdin Sane* and *Let's Dance*. Bowie earned $55 million from the venture.

> **"I THINK THE POTENTIAL OF WHAT THE INTERNET IS GOING TO DO TO SOCIETY, BOTH GOOD AND BAD, IS UNIMAGINABLE."**

—David Bowie,
*Newsnight*, BBC, 1999

## BOWIENET

In 1998, Bowie became the first musician to launch their own Internet service provider. For a small subscription fee, BowieNet users could create their own email address, access news and photo archives, listen to music and watch videos.

## FACE OF FINANCE

In 2000, Bowie set up his own branded online bank, BowieBanc. The bank issued its customers with debit cards and cheques featuring the star's face. A one-year subscription to BowieNet was included with the account as an added bonus.

# 5 THINGS YOU DIDN'T KNOW ABOUT BOWIE

**1** Bowie fainted with fear when a plane he was travelling on was struck by lightning. For many years afterwards Bowie chose to travel overseas by boat. In 1972, Bowie took a cabin on the *Queen Elizabeth 2* to New York for his tour of the USA.

**2** Bowie was never known for his domestic prowess and claims he wasn't much of a cook either: "I burn water … Oh, I could boil an egg. And make radioactive coffee." His favourite meal was a taste of Britain – Iman's home-cooked shepherd's pie.

**3** Bowie often read a book a day. He had a great sense of humour and enjoyed the comic *Viz* as well as Spike Milligan's *Puckoon*. On a more serious note, he rated R. D. Laing's *The Divided Self*. Fiction such as Nabokov's *Lolita* and *Black Boy* by Richard Wright were favourites, too.

**4** In 1969, Bowie appeared in an advert for Lyons Maid Luv ice cream. The director was a young film-maker called Ridley Scott, who would later go on to direct *Alien* and *Gladiator*.

**5** Bowie was asked to sing on the Queen song 'Cool Cat' from the 1982 album *Hot Space*, but, unhappy with his vocals, dismissed the track. He proceeded to jam with the band, and wrote the Number 1 single 'Under Pressure'.

# DAVID BOWIE

## 03
### WORK

"I HAD TO RESIGN MYSELF, MANY YEARS AGO, THAT I'M NOT TOO ARTICULATE WHEN IT COMES TO EXPLAINING HOW I FEEL ABOUT THINGS. BUT MY MUSIC DOES IT FOR ME, IT REALLY DOES. THERE, IN THE CHORDS AND MELODIES, IS EVERYTHING I WANT TO SAY."

—David Bowie, *Livewire*, 16 June 2002

# THE MOMENT THAT MOVED A GENERATION: 6 JULY 1972

**0:01** Opening close-up of a blue 12-string guitar as Bowie's fingers strum the opening bars of 'Starman'.

**0:16** Cut to show Bowie's impish grin and his red bottle-brush hair – glam rock is all the rage, but this is something else ...

**0:21** Pull out slowly to reveal Bowie's technicoloured jumpsuit.

**0:37** Pan out to the rest of the band. The drummer is wearing silky pink, and Mick Ronson, with his peroxide long hair, is in a gold jumpsuit.

| PROGRAMME: | SONG: | VIEWERS: |
| --- | --- | --- |
| *TOP OF THE POPS* | **'STARMAN'** | **15** MILLION |

**1:38** Bowie directs his gaze forwards, and as he sings he points his finger at the camera as if he's addressing each viewer.

**2:17** Bowie drapes his arm around guitarist Mick Ronson. Is it a gesture of friendship or suggestive of something more?

**3:20** Cut to boy in tank top and girls dancing awkwardly. The juxtaposition between the band of aliens and gawky youths is a statement in itself.

WORK

# ANATOMY OF AN LP: HUNKY DORY

David Bowie's fourth studio album, and his first for RCA Records, was the record where his ability as a songwriter really began to show. His previous album, *The Man Who Sold the World*, had been a minor success – though not successful enough to chart – but it was experimental and inconsistent. Released just over a year later, *Hunky Dory* was a critical and commercial hit immediately and is still regarded as one of Bowie's finest works. In 2010, *Time* magazine included the record in its '100 best albums of all time'.

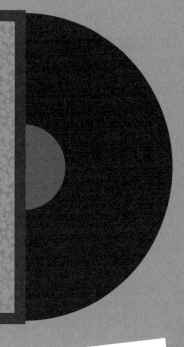

## 5 HUNKY DORY STORIES

1. **'Queen Bitch' was written as a tribute to Lou Reed and The Velvet Underground.**
2. **The piano played by Rick Wakeman was a 100-year-old Beckstein and was also used on songs by The Beatles, Elton John and Genesis.**
3. **Bowie often told different stories on the meaning behind 'The Bewlay Brothers', but finally admitted that it was in reference to his half-brother Terry, who had battled with schizophrenia.**
4. **Bowie's son was born a week before the album sessions began.**
5. **The album cover art was inspired by photographs of Marlene Dietrich.**

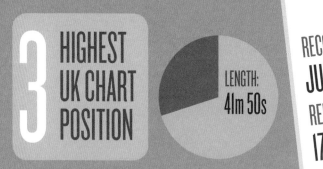

**3** HIGHEST UK CHART POSITION

LENGTH: 41m 50s

RECORDED: JUNE – AUGUST 1971

RELEASED: 17 DECEMBER 1971

# THE PLAYERS

### DAVID BOWIE

### MICK RONSON

### TREVOR BOLDER

### MICK WOODMANSEY

### RICK WAKEMAN

### KEN SCOTT
**Production**

# TRACK LISTING

I. CHANGES
2. OH! YOU PRETTY THINGS
3. EIGHT LINE POEM
4. LIFE ON MARS?
5. KOOKS
6. QUICKSAND
7. FILL YOUR HEART
8. ANDY WARHOL
9. SONG FOR BOB DYLAN
10. QUEEN BITCH
11. THE BEWLAY BROTHERS

## THEMES

- American heroes
- Fatherhood and family
- It's a hippy folk thing
- Out of this world

The album was recorded at Trident Studios, London.

## MAJOR TOM

Created in 1969, the same year as the moon landing, Major Tom was a fictional astronaut and a semi-autobiographical outlet for Bowie. Major Tom was a lost soul battling with addiction.

## ARNOLD CORNS

In 1971, along with fashion designer Freddie Burretti, Bowie recorded a number of tracks for B&C Records. At the time, Bowie was still under contract with Mercury and unable to release them under his own name, and so Arnold Corns was born. The side project was not a success.

## ZIGGY STARDUST

Bowie's iconic alter ego was an androgynous, bisexual, glam-rock, red-haired alien. First appearing in February 1972, Bowie became totally immersed in the character. In 1973, after two albums and less than 18 months from conception, Bowie retired Ziggy.

# THE MANY FACES OF DAVID BOWIE

# ALADDIN SANE

Although Aladdin Sane (a pun on A Lad Insane) was an independent character, Bowie saw him as merely an evolution of Ziggy Stardust. Created for the 1973 album of the same name, Bowie once described the character as "Ziggy goes to America" and he was even more in your face and shocking than Ziggy.

# HALLOWEEN JACK

Having left Ziggy Stardust and Aladdin Sane behind, in 1974 Bowie moved to the USA and transformed himself again. Halloween Jack was "a real cool cat" who debuted on Bowie's 1974 album, *Diamond Dogs*. The spiky hair, eye patch and scarf were precursors of the punk-rock look.

# THE THIN WHITE DUKE

Impeccably dressed, desensitized and amoral, Bowie described the Thin White Duke, his persona in 1975–6, as "a nasty character indeed". With his hair groomed and wearing a crisp white shirt and waistcoat, the Thin White Duke was in complete contrast to his previous incarnations, though no less outrageous. Bowie later apologized for some of his actions as the Duke.

# FASHION EVOLUTION

Experimentation and change were integral to Bowie's music, life and look. Ever-evolving, yet always interesting, his wardrobe was as much part of the act as his music ...

## 1960s MOD

Sixties' London was mobbed with mods and Bowie embraced the look with boxy jackets and mohair suits.

## DRESS TO THRILL

Bowie had long, flowing hair and a penchant for androgynous clothes and bell bottoms.

## FAR OUT

Angie Bowie helped invent the outlandish outfits for Ziggy Stardust and Aladdin Sane. Designer Freddie Burretti styled much of the look, including the famous quilted jumpsuits.

## TOKYO POP

Bowie worked with fashion designer Kansai Yamamoto for his Aladdin Sane wardrobe. This Space Samurai outfit, with its loose martial art trousers, is iconic.

## SUITS YOU

Freddie Burretti was back in wardrobe to design the pale-blue suit and distinctive blue jumper worn by Bowie on the Diamond Dogs Tour of 1974.

## MODERN LOVE

This Union Jack coat was designed for Bowie by Alexander McQueen. Bowie wore the coat on the cover of his 1997 album, *Earthling*.

# ANATOMY OF AN LP: "HEROES"

In 1976, Bowie swapped Los Angeles for Berlin in a bid to quit cocaine and avoid the limelight. While sharing an apartment with Iggy Pop, Bowie became interested in the German music scene and the minimal sounds of Brian Eno. The 'Berlin Trilogy', Bowie's collaborations with Eno, defined Bowie in the 1970s as experimental and progressive. *"Heroes"* is considered a creative peak with Bowie's striking vocals, Eno's synthesizers and Robert Fripp's guitars – enhanced by Visconti's innovative production – going on to influence a generation of musicians.

## 5 "HEROES" STORIES

1. Visconti set up three microphones (instead of the usual one) to record the vocals: at 9 inches (23 cm), 20 feet (6 m) and 50 feet (15 m).
2. Bowie said that the quotation marks in the title "indicate a dimension of irony about the word 'heroes' or about the whole concept of heroism".
3. The studio was 547 yards (500 m) from the Berlin Wall.
4. 'Oblique Strategies' was a set of cards created by Brian Eno and used by Bowie. Through picking a card and following the instructions, an artist could overcome a creative block.
5. The song "Heroes" tells the story of two lovers and was inspired by producer Tony Visconti kissing his girlfriend at the Berlin Wall.

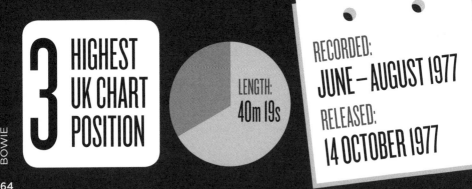

**3** HIGHEST UK CHART POSITION

LENGTH: 40m 19s

RECORDED: JUNE – AUGUST 1977

RELEASED: 14 OCTOBER 1977

# THE PLAYERS

## DAVID BOWIE

## ROBERT FRIPP

## CARLOS ALOMAR

## DENNIS DAVIS

## BRIAN ENO

## TONY VISCONTI
Production, percussion
and backing vocals

# TRACK LISTING

1. BEAUTY AND THE BEAST
2. JOE THE LION
3. "HEROES"
4. SONS OF THE SILENT AGE
5. BLACKOUT
6. V-2 SCHNEIDER
7. SENSE OF DOUBT
8. MOSS GARDEN
9. NEUKÖLN
10. THE SECRET LIFE OF ARABIA

## THEMES

- Love story
- Oblique strategy
- Cocaine addiction/ survival/madness
- Instrumental

The album was recorded at
Hansa Tonstudios, Berlin.

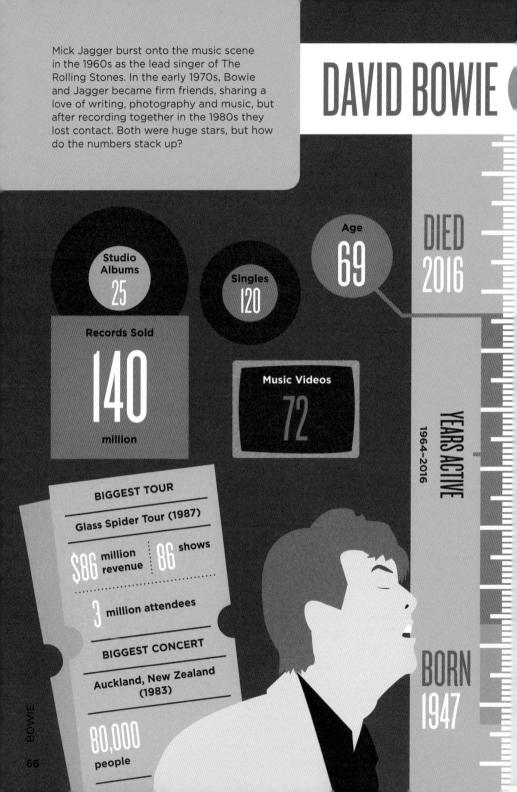

Mick Jagger burst onto the music scene in the 1960s as the lead singer of The Rolling Stones. In the early 1970s, Bowie and Jagger became firm friends, sharing a love of writing, photography and music, but after recording together in the 1980s they lost contact. Both were huge stars, but how do the numbers stack up?

# DAVID BOWIE

**DIED**
**2016**

**Age**
**69**

**Studio Albums**
**25**

**Singles**
**120**

**Records Sold**
**140**
**million**

**Music Videos**
**72**

**YEARS ACTIVE**
1964–2016

**BIGGEST TOUR**

Glass Spider Tour (1987)

**$86** million revenue  :  **86** shows

**3** million attendees

**BIGGEST CONCERT**

Auckland, New Zealand (1983)

**80,000** people

**BORN**
**1947**

# MICK JAGGER

## DANCING IN THE STREET

In 1985, Bowie and Jagger covered the 1964 Marvin Gaye song 'Dancing in the Street' for Live Aid. The single was a huge success and went to number one in the UK charts.

**YEARS ACTIVE**

1962–

**BORN**

**1943**

Singles
**120**

Studio Albums
**30**

Music Videos
**64**

Records Sold
**140**
million

BIGGEST TOUR

A Bigger Bang (2005-7)

**$558** million revenue

**147** shows

**4.68** million attendees

BIGGEST CONCERT

Rio de Janeiro, Brazil (2006)

**1,500,000** people

# ROCK 'N' ROLL WITH ME?

Bowie loved working with other musicians and encouraged creativity and experimentation in the studio. When he got together with Queen in 1981 to record 'Under Pressure', Bowie led the way with the lyrics and opening riff. It was a number one hit in the UK for the king of collaboration. So who else did Bowie hook up with?

STEVIE RAY VAUGHAN

QUEEN

PETE TOWNSHEND

EARL SLICK

TONY VISCONTI

MICK RONSON

LOU REED

RICK WAKEMAN

ROBERT FRIPP

# ANATOMY OF AN LP: BLACKSTAR

David Bowie's final studio album was recorded in secret in the spring of 2015 and released on Bowie's 69th birthday on 8 January 2016. Two days later, Bowie passed away. Even though the themes of the album seemingly grapple with Bowie's own mortality, Bowie was full of energy and in good spirits during the recording. Guitarist Ben Monder remembered: "I would leave the studio every day in a state of elation. I certainly had no idea I would be participating in his final project. There was a darkness to some of the material, but I never read anything too dire into it."

## 5 BLACKSTAR SECRETS

1. The cover, label and album sleeve are the work of Jonathan Barnbrook, who also designed *Heathen*, *Reality* and *The Next Day*.
2. The album is filled with mysteries and secrets, including stars that appear on the album itself when it is held in direct sunlight.
3. The star segments on the cover, below the main star, spell out the word BOWIE.
4. *Blackstar* became the first number one album for Bowie in the USA.
5. It is the first of Bowie's albums not to feature his portrait on the cover.

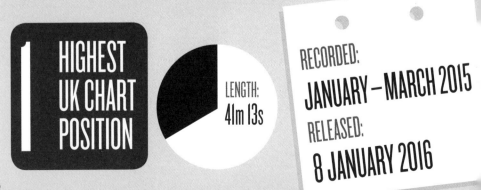

**1** HIGHEST UK CHART POSITION

LENGTH: 41m 13s

RECORDED: JANUARY – MARCH 2015

RELEASED: 8 JANUARY 2016

# THE PLAYERS

### DAVID BOWIE

### DONNY MCCASLIN

### BEN MONDER

### TIM LEFEBVRE

### MARK GUILIANA

### JASON LINDNER

**TONY VISCONTI**
**Production, strings**
**and engineering**

# TRACK LISTING

1. **BLACKSTAR**
2. **'TIS A PITY SHE WAS A WHORE**
3. **LAZARUS**
4. **SUE (OR IN A SEASON OF CRIME)**
5. **GIRL LOVES ME**
6. **DOLLAR DAYS**
7. **I CAN'T GIVE EVERYTHING AWAY**

## THEMES

● Murder (based on a play)

● First World War

● Pain and medication use

○ Farewell and death

The album was recorded at the Magic Shop and Human Worldwide Studios in New York.

WORK

THE MAN WHO SOLD THE WORLD
1970

DIAMOND DOGS
1974

LOW
1977

DAVID BOWIE
1967

THE RISE AND FALL OF ZIGGY STARDUST AND THE SPIDERS FROM MARS
1972

YOUNG AMERICANS
1975

# THE ALBUMS

In November 2016, *Legacy: The Best of Bowie* was released. It's an easy way into the music of Bowie. However, to really understand the man and his music there are 25 studio albums to explore ...

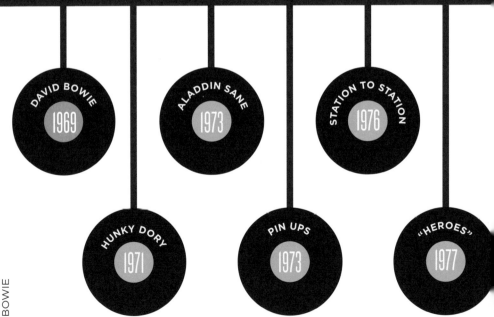

DAVID BOWIE
1969

ALADDIN SANE
1973

STATION TO STATION
1976

HUNKY DORY
1971

PIN UPS
1973

"HEROES"
1977

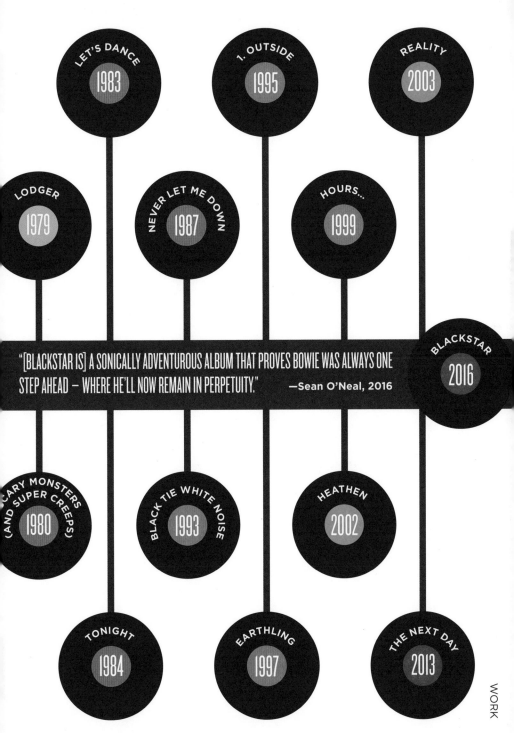

LET'S DANCE
1983

1. OUTSIDE
1995

REALITY
2003

LODGER
1979

NEVER LET ME DOWN
1987

HOURS...
1999

BLACKSTAR
2016

"[BLACKSTAR IS] A SONICALLY ADVENTUROUS ALBUM THAT PROVES BOWIE WAS ALWAYS ONE STEP AHEAD — WHERE HE'LL NOW REMAIN IN PERPETUITY." —Sean O'Neal, 2016

SCARY MONSTERS (AND SUPER CREEPS)
1980

BLACK TIE WHITE NOISE
1993

HEATHEN
2002

TONIGHT
1984

EARTHLING
1997

THE NEXT DAY
2013

# THE ART OF WRITING SONGS

CUT

UP...

> "I FORCED MYSELF TO BECOME A GOOD SONGWRITER – AND I BECAME A GOOD SONGWRITER. I MADE A JOB OF WORK AT GETTING GOOD."
>
> —David Bowie, *Starman*, 2012

Bowie began using a 'cut up' method for writing songs in the mid-1970s. The idea was inspired by author William S. Burroughs who had employed the technique when writing his novel *Naked Lunch*. Bowie took the lyrics that he'd written on paper and cut them into small sections that he could shuffle and rearrange into something more intriguing.

## PIANO MAN ...

Angie Bowie was living with Bowie at Haddon Hall when he composed the songs for *Hunky Dory* and *The Rise and Fall of Ziggy Stardust and the Spiders from Mars*. She remembers him spending hours at the piano: "David is a fantastic musician because his approach is not studied, it's by ear. He has an ability to pluck a song from those first moments when he plays with an instrument. Writing on the piano opened up his possibilities, because of its association with so many kinds of music – classical, cabaret, every style."

# DAVID BOWIE

## 04
### LEGACY

"DURAN DURAN, MADONNA, LADY GAGA, BEYONCÉ, DAFT PUNK — WHENEVER POP IS AMBITIOUS, WHENEVER POP IS ODD, WHENEVER POP DRESSES UP, WHENEVER POP LOOKS LIKE NOTHING YOU'VE SEEN BEFORE, IT IS USING TOOLS AND A FRAMEWORK LARGELY BUILT BY ONE MAN FROM BROMLEY WITH TOMBSTONE TEETH, AND HIS NAME BORROWED FROM A FIXED-BLADE FIGHTING KNIFE."

—Caitlin Moran, *Moranifesto*, 2016

# BOWIE IN NUMBERS

## 25 STUDIO ALBUMS

## 5 GRAMMY AWARDS

Bowie also won a Lifetime Achievement Award in 2006.

## 11 UK NO. 1 ALBUMS

*Aladdin Sane, Pin Ups, Diamond Dogs, Scary Monsters (And Super Creeps), Let's Dance, Tonight, Changesbowie, Black Tie White Noise, Best of Bowie, The Next Day, Blackstar*

## 4 BRIT AWARDS

Bowie also won the Outstanding Contribution to British Music Icon in 1996, and the Icon Award in 2016.

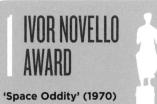

# IVOR NOVELLO AWARD

'Space Oddity' (1970)

## 5 UK NO. 1 SINGLES

'Space Oddity', 'Ashes to Ashes', 'Under Pressure', 'Let's Dance', 'Dancing in the Street'

# 120 SINGLES

# IS THERE ANY CH-CH-CHANGE?

## WORLD'S MOST EXPENSIVE MUSIC VIDEOS (BY YEAR)

| $7,000,000 |
| $6,500,000 |
| $6,000,000 |
| $5,500,000 |
| $5,000,000 |
| $4,500,000 |
| $4,000,000 |
| $3,500,000 |
| $3,000,000 |
| $2,500,000 |
| $2,000,000 |
| $1,500,000 |
| $1,000,000 |
| $500,000 |

| 1980 | 1983 | 1987 | 1989 |
|------|------|------|------|
| **David Bowie** 'Ashes to Ashes' | **Michael Jackson** 'Thriller' | **Michael Jackson** 'Bad' | **Madonna** 'Express Yourself' |

Bowie had a soft spot for his first creation, Major Tom of 'Space Oddity', so he continued with his story in the song 'Ashes to Ashes' from the album *Scary Monsters (And Super Creeps)*. The music video, filmed on the south coast of England with a cast of oddballs including Steve Strange of Visage and costumes designed by Natasha Korniloff, cost a staggering $500,000 – the most expensive music video ever made at the time.

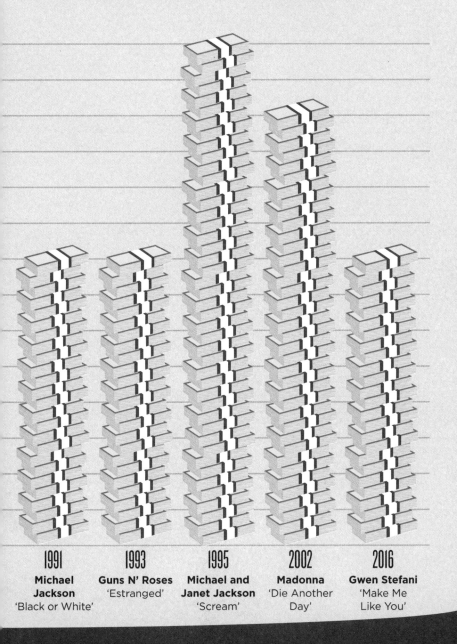

| 1991 | 1993 | 1995 | 2002 | 2016 |
|---|---|---|---|---|
| **Michael Jackson** 'Black or White' | **Guns N' Roses** 'Estranged' | **Michael and Janet Jackson** 'Scream' | **Madonna** 'Die Another Day' | **Gwen Stefani** 'Make Me Like You' |

# OPENING DOORS

Bowie made music in a wide variety of styles, and produced memorable songs in all of them. He opened the door for millions of people from all kinds of background and influenced more musical genres than anyone else.

## PUNK

Siouxsie Sioux once said that punk wouldn't have happened without Bowie. Through Bowie, young punks got to Iggy Pop, credited as the 'Godfather of Punk'. "He was the most important artist of the 20th century," said Siouxsie.

## POP

Paul Weller said the drums alone on 'Sound and Vision' defined the sound of drums for the next decade, while *Low* married the avant-garde with a lyrical and melodic style that has shaped the sound of modern pop music ever since.

## INDIE

Bowie made it OK to be different. Ian McCulloch of Echo and the Bunnymen (below) was inspired by this philosophy. In his song 'Me and David Bowie', he tried to explain and say thank you to his hero.

## POST-PUNK

Joy Division and breakaway band New Order are indebted to Bowie for the experimental sounds he delivered in his album *Low*. David Gahan of Depeche Mode grew up thinking he was going nowhere in life, but Bowie gave him faith to escape ...

## NEW ROMANTIC

Duran Duran, Spandau Ballet and Japan borrowed Bowie's look and Bowie took it right back in the video for 'Ashes to Ashes'.

## ROCK

U2's the Edge claimed that Bowie's "restless creative spirit" gave them the strength to release records such as *Achtung Baby*. Johnny Marr of The Smiths once said that Bowie showed how you could be anything you wanted to be by acting like you believed it.

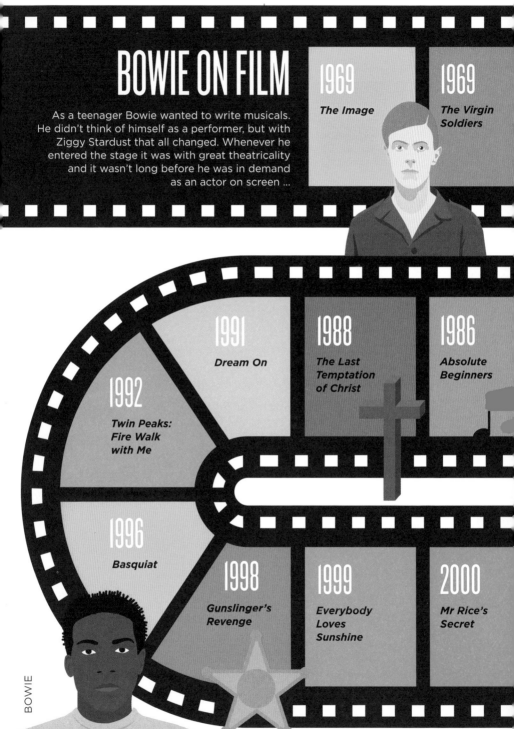

# BOWIE ON FILM

As a teenager Bowie wanted to write musicals. He didn't think of himself as a performer, but with Ziggy Stardust that all changed. Whenever he entered the stage it was with great theatricality and it wasn't long before he was in demand as an actor on screen ...

## 1969
*The Image*

## 1969
*The Virgin Soldiers*

## 1991
*Dream On*

## 1988
*The Last Temptation of Christ*

## 1986
*Absolute Beginners*

## 1992
*Twin Peaks: Fire Walk with Me*

## 1996
*Basquiat*

## 1998
*Gunslinger's Revenge*

## 1999
*Everybody Loves Sunshine*

## 2000
*Mr Rice's Secret*

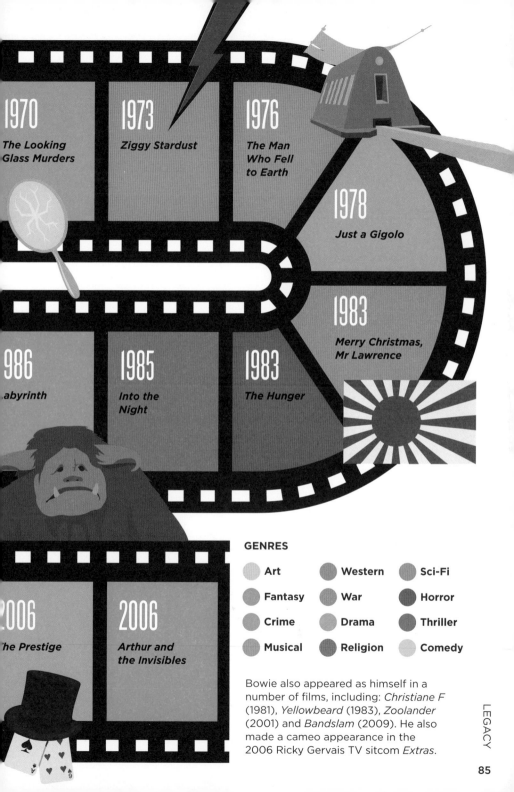

**1970**

The Looking
Glass Murders

**1973**

Ziggy Stardust

**1976**

The Man
Who Fell
to Earth

**1978**

Just a Gigolo

**1983**

Merry Christmas,
Mr Lawrence

**986**

abyrinth

**1985**

Into the
Night

**1983**

The Hunger

**2006**

he Prestige

**2006**

Arthur and
the Invisibles

**GENRES**

- Art
- Fantasy
- Crime
- Musical
- Western
- War
- Drama
- Religion
- Sci-Fi
- Horror
- Thriller
- Comedy

Bowie also appeared as himself in a
number of films, including: *Christiane F*
(1981), *Yellowbeard* (1983), *Zoolander*
(2001) and *Bandslam* (2009). He also
made a cameo appearance in the
2006 Ricky Gervais TV sitcom *Extras*.

LEGACY

# 42 WORDS

In 2013, when Bowie was asked by a journalist to supply a workflow diagram for his latest album *The Next Day*, he responded with 42 words …

SUCCUBUS

INDULGENCES

INTIMIDATION

VAMPYRIC

TRANSFERENCE

ISOLATION

VIOLENCE

PANTHEON

HOSTAGE

CHTHONIC

IDENTITY

EFFIGIES

REVENGE

INTERFACE

OSMOSIS

CRUSADE

FLITTING

TYRANT

DOMINATION

BURIAL

TRACE

GLIDE

FLIGHT

PRESSGANG

INDIFFERENCE

RESETTLEMENT

ANARCHIST

TRAITOR

MANIPULATE

REVERSE

MIASMA

DISPLACED

FUNEREAL

ORIGIN

COMEUPPANCE

BALKAN

MAUER

URBAN

MYSTIFICATION

TRAGIC

NERVE

TEXT

# AUCTION OF BOWIE'S ESTATE

When he died, Bowie left most of his estate of about $100 million to Iman and his children. On 10–11 November 2016, over 400 works owned by Bowie, including art and furniture, were put up for auction at Sotheby's in London.

## ART

**356**
Total number of art lots

**£14.3m**
Predicted sales

**£32.9m**
Total actual sales

59 ARTISTS, WHOSE WORK WAS INCLUDED IN BOWIE'S COLLECTION, HAD RECORDS SET FOR THE SALE OF THEIR WORK

**40,000** = 1,000

people viewed the sale over 10 days. Almost 3,000 potential buyers from 46 different countries registered to bid.

# DESIGN

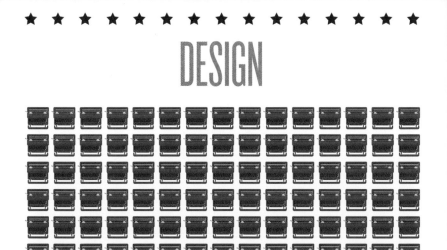

## 1 FOR THE PRICE OF 150

A red Olivetti Valentine typewriter, designed by Sottsass and Perry King, was valued at £300 but sold to a telephone bidder for £45,000 pounds, 150 times the estimate.

## $323,049

**Price paid for Bowie's custom Brionvega record player**

### £117k

**Predicted sales**

### £1.4m

**Total actual sales**

## THE RECORD PLAYER WAS VALUED AT BETWEEN £1,000 AND £2,000.

# 5 THINGS NAMED AFTER BOWIE

## SEVEN STARS

To celebrate the life of the 'Starman', a group of Belgian astronomers looked up to the heavens for inspiration. They claimed that seven stars in the vicinity of Mars shone brightly and formed a constellation in the shape of the Aladdin Sane lightning bolt. It isn't official, but an application for naming the constellation after Bowie has been made.

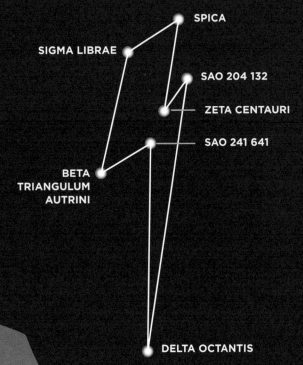

SPICA

SIGMA LIBRAE

SAO 204 132

ZETA CENTAURI

SAO 241 641

BETA TRIANGULUM AUTRINI

DELTA OCTANTIS

## 342843 DAVIDBOWIE

Just three days before Bowie's 68th birthday, the Minor Planet Center, an organization for observing minor planets, approved the naming of a small asteroid after the singer. It was first discovered in 2008 by German astronomer Felix Hormuth.

## SPIDER-MAN

A bright-yellow huntsman spider, discovered in 2009 in Malaysia, was named *Heteropoda davidbowie*.

## BLACKSTAR GELATO

In 2017, an ice-cream parlour in Berlin revealed their newest gelato, 'Black Star'. Named after Bowie's final album, it was created by combining chestnut ice cream with dark chocolate and a cream flavoured with Cuban cigar smoke.

## BRIXTON POUND

The Brixton Pound, a local London currency, was created in 2009 to encourage trade. In 2011, the £10 note commemorating the 'Brixton boy' was unveiled. On Bowie's death, banknotes were changing hands for up to five times their value.

10

BRIXTON£

# BIOGRAPHIES

## Iggy Pop (1947–)

Iggy Pop called Bowie's friendship "the light of my life". The two met in 1971, and by 1976 Bowie had taken the drug-addled Iggy under his wing, and produced and collaborated on his first album, *The Idiot*. Iggy later moved into Bowie's Berlin apartment.

## Lou Reed (1942–2013)

Bowie called Reed the "master" and in the 1960s Bowie was enamoured of The Velvet Underground. Bowie co-produced Reed's second solo-album, *Transformer*, and they remained friends until Reed's death in 2013.

## Kate Moss (1974–)

Kate Moss saw Bowie as a father figure. They became friends after a photo shoot for Q magazine in 2003. In 2014, Moss wore Bowie's iconic 'Woodland Creatures' outfit to accept the BRIT award for Best Male Solo Artist on his behalf.

## Tony Visconti (1944–)

The American record producer and musician worked on 13 of Bowie's albums. Their friendship deepened over the years, despite their occasional differences. Visconti was one of the few in the inner circle of friends who knew about Bowie's illness.

## Robert Fox (1952–)

The English film and theatre director became friends with Bowie in 1974. They bonded over books and the theatre, and remained close for more than 40 years. Their final project was working on the musical *Lazarus* together.

## Coco (Corinne) Schwab

Bowie's personal assistant for 43 years, Schwab started as an office girl for Bowie's management company in 1973. Within six months she was Bowie's personal assistant and accompanied him on all his tours. Bowie once said that Schwab was his best friend.

### Marc Bolan
### (1947–77)

Bowie met Marc Bolan in the 1960s while working as a decorator. In 1971, Bolan became famous with T. Rex after the hit 'Ride a White Swan'. Bowie appeared on the final *Marc* show in September 1977 – within the month Bolan had been killed in a car crash.

### Tilda Swinton
### (1960–)

"He looked like someone from the same planet as me," said Swinton, who met and became friends with Bowie when he rang her to appear alongside him in the 2013 video for 'The Stars (Are Out Tonight)'. The actress said he felt like a cousin and they remained close.

### George Underwood
### (1947–)

George was Bowie's oldest friend and the reason for his mismatched eyes. Underwood is best known as an artist and for designing album covers in the 1970s, including *Hunky Dory* and *The Rise and Fall of Ziggy Stardust and the Spiders from Mars*.

### John Lennon
### (1940–80)

Bowie and the ex-Beatle met for the first time in 1974. They collaborated on 'Fame', which went on to become Bowie's first US number one single. In his final interview, Lennon said he wanted to record something as good as Bowie's *"Heroes"*.

### Mick Ronson
### (1946–93)

Bowie's guitarist hailed from Kingston upon Hull. He was known for his guitar solos but also orchestrated the string section on Lou Reed's 'Walk on the Wild Side'. He died young and slightly unsung from liver cancer.

### Brian Eno
### (1948–)

The English musician and composer was a friend and collaborator for more than 40 years, working with Bowie on *Low*, *"Heroes"*, *Lodger* and *Outside*. Eno remembers Bowie's humorous emails, including his final one: "Thank you for our good times, Brian. They will never rot."

musician          producer

friend            assistant

# INDEX

# BOWIE IN NUMBERS

## 25 STUDIO ALBUMS

### 11 UK NO 1 ALBUMS

*Aladdin Sane, Pin Ups, Diamond Dogs, Scary Monsters (And Super Creeps), Let's Dance, Tonight, Changesbowie, Black Tie White Noise, Best of Bowie, The Next Day, Blackstar*

## 5 GRAMMY AWARDS

## 4 BRIT AWARDS

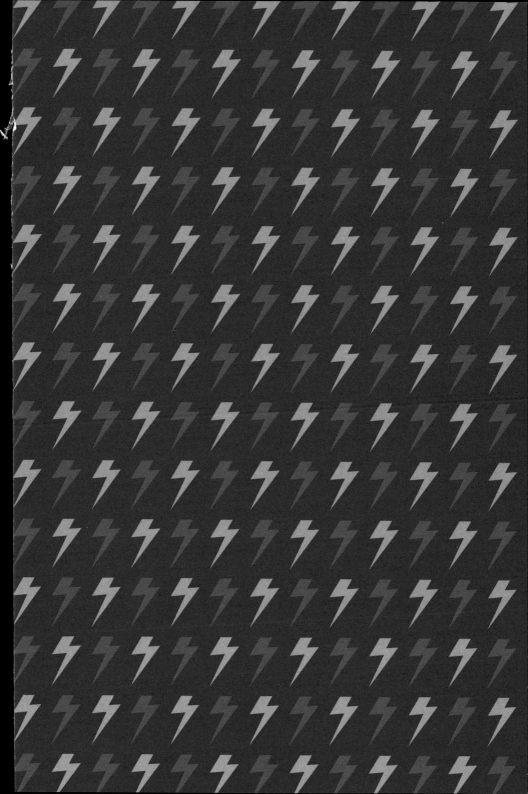

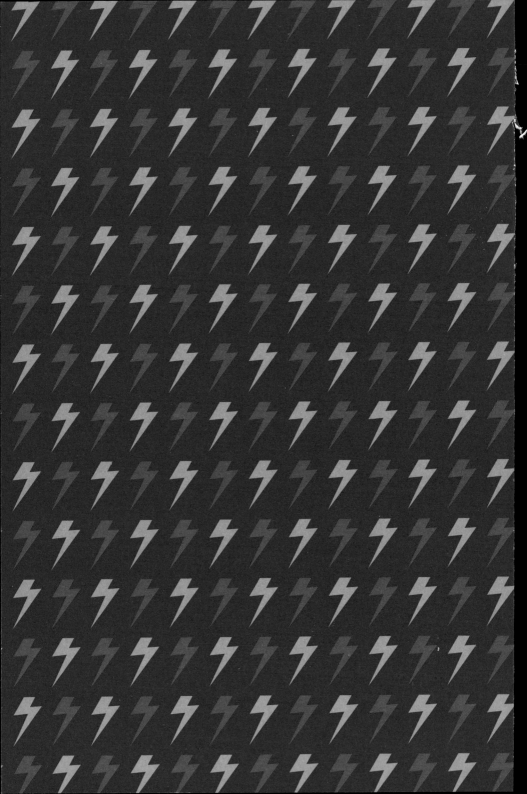